CANDY & SHELLEY GO TO THE DESERT

BY PAULA CIZMAR

DRAMATISTS
PLAY SERVICE
INC.

CANDY & SHELLEY GO TO THE DESERT
Copyright © 1988, Paula Cizmar
Copyright © 1984, Paula Cizmar
as an unpublished dramatic composition

All Rights Reserved

CAUTION: Professionals and amateurs are hereby warned that performance of CANDY & SHELLEY GO TO THE DESERT is subject to payment of a royalty. It is fully protected under the copyright laws of the United States of America, and of all countries covered by the International Copyright Union (including the Dominion of Canada and the rest of the British Commonwealth), and of all countries covered by the Pan-American Copyright Convention, the Universal Copyright Convention, the Berne Convention, and of all countries with which the United States has reciprocal copyright relations. All rights, including professional/amateur stage rights, motion picture, recitation, lecturing, public reading, radio broadcasting, television, video or sound recording, all other forms of mechanical or electronic reproduction, such as CD-ROM, CD-I, DVD, information storage and retrieval systems and photocopying, and the rights of translation into foreign languages, are strictly reserved. Particular emphasis is placed upon the matter of readings, permission for which must be secured from the Author's agent in writing.

The English language stock and amateur stage performance rights in the United States, its territories, possessions and Canada for CANDY & SHELLEY GO TO THE DESERT are controlled exclusively by DRAMATISTS PLAY SERVICE, INC., 440 Park Avenue South, New York, NY 10016. No professional or nonprofessional performance of the Play may be given without obtaining in advance the written permission of DRAMATISTS PLAY SERVICE, INC., and paying the requisite fee.

Inquiries concerning all other rights should be addressed to William Morris Agency, Inc., 1325 Avenue of the Americas, 15th Floor, New York, NY 10019.

SPECIAL NOTE
Anyone receiving permission to produce CANDY & SHELLEY GO TO THE DESERT is required to give credit to the Author as sole and exclusive Author of the Play on the title page of all programs distributed in connection with performances of the Play and in all instances in which the title of the Play appears for purposes of advertising, publicizing or otherwise exploiting the Play and/or a production thereof. The name of the Author must appear on a separate line, in which no other name appears, immediately beneath the title and in size of type equal to 50% of the size of the largest, most prominent letter used for the title of the Play. No person, firm or entity may receive credit larger or more prominent than that accorded the Author. The following acknowledgment must appear on the title page in all programs distributed in connection with performances of the Play:

Originally produced as part of the Women's Project
at the American Place Theatre.

SPECIAL NOTE ON SONGS AND RECORDINGS
For performances of copyrighted songs, arrangements or recordings mentioned in this Play, the permission of the copyright owner(s) must be obtained. Other songs, arrangements or recordings may be substituted provided permission from the copyright owner(s) of such songs, arrangements or recordings is obtained; or songs, arrangements or recordings in the public domain may be substituted.

An earlier version of this play was produced by The Women's Project on the mainstage of the American Place Theatre in New York City as part of a festival of one-acts.

CANDY & SHELLEY GO TO THE DESERT, in this revised form, was produced in London, England by Theatre La Beet at the Old Red Lion Theatre, opening May 20, 1986, with a subsequent run at the Croydon Warehouse Theatre, London.

Directed by Terry Johnson
Scenic and costume design by Antony Ward
Lighting by Andy Wilson

Cast:
CANDY............................... Zaro Weil
SHELLEY........................ Charon Bourke
RON (THE BIKER)................. Nick Dunning

CANDY & SHELLEY GO TO THE DESERT was subsequently presented by Georgia Bragg and Valri Jackson at Theatre West, in Los Angeles, California, opening August 9, 1987.

Directed by Michael Barker
Scenic and lighting design by David Taylor

Cast:
CANDY....................... Catherine MacNeal
SHELLEY..................... Melinda Peterson
RON (THE BIKER).................... Casey King

CHARACTERS

CANDY. A young woman, formerly from Indiana, now locked into the Big Apple. She is sensibly dressed for travel, possibly shorts, a loose shirt, running shoes.

SHELLEY. A young woman, native of New York and still there. She does not have the first notion of what to wear on a cross-country trip; she's possibly attired in tight pants and a halter top (or an urban-looking sundress) with a blouse tied at the waist, and high heeled sandals.

RON (THE BIKER). A young man from Michigan, in black helmet, mirrored shades, and black leather from head to toe.

Time
The present. August.

Place
The desert.

CANDY & SHELLEY GO TO THE DESERT

SCENE: The Desert. A sparsely traveled desert road, no more than two lanes, about 60 miles south of Elko, Nevada — just off I-80. The location is specific, but it need not be. One hellhole in Nevada is pretty much the same as the next.

This is a typical desert with typical desert furnishings: washed out sandy clay soil, sagebrush, pebbles, a few nondescript cacti, a beer can, a lot of sky — dusty, but cloudless. Off in the distance are jagged, lifeless rock formations, cracking out of the ground.

A boulder Center is large enough to lie on — but in the heat and light of this August day, it creates nothing as humane as shade.

PRESHOW: We hear noise and music from a car radio. A Nevada DJ drawls on about a local livestock judging event . . . entries from five northern Nevada counties . . . including a new entry this year from the Duck Valley Reservation . . . and we wish them well . . . Right now it's 113 degrees in the shade in downtown Elko . . . so all you lonesome cowboys out there on the bubbling blacktop, why don't you pull on into the Washoe Mountain Truck Stop . . . have yourself an ice cold cherry pop or something . . . we'll keep you company right here . . . all your favorite tunes . . . The DJ spins a record — something desultory, mysterious, as hot as the desert itself, like the Eagles' "Journey to the Sorcerer" or something of Ry Cooder's.*

As the houselights dim, we hear a car with a growling muffler approach and screech to a halt. The driver lays on the horn, throws a door open, slams it shut.

---

*See Special Note on copyright page.
Or, see also alternative pre-show Disc Jockey material on pages following this play.

CANDY. *(Candy runs onstage.)* Ohmygod, out! Get outa the car! Shelley! Please just for once do what I say. *(Candy runs off again. We hear a bit of commotion, sounds of struggle. Offstage:)* Shelley! Please. Come on. Wake up! Get out!
SHELLEY. *(Offstage.)* Hey. What . . . Stop it . . . Candy . . . *(Candy drags Shelley onstage, holding her arm in a tight grip.)*
CANDY. Come on . . . run . . . let's go. Hurry. Behind the rock!
SHELLEY. *(Overlapping.)* You're hurting my—hey, what's wrong—rock? Rock? *(Candy pushes Shelley down behind the rock—they face the audience.)* Oh. Rock.
CANDY. Get down quick.
SHELLEY. Nice rock. It's a really pretty rock. *(She starts to stand up; Candy pushes her back down.)* Candy!
CANDY. Now stay down and please, for God's sake, keep quiet.
SHELLEY. What? What's going on? Candy?
CANDY. Sshh. It's gonna blow up.
SHELLEY. What is? What—
CANDY. Sshh!
SHELLEY. What's my making noise got to do with—?
CANDY. Sshhh. I'm warning you.
SHELLEY. Candy—
CANDY. Things travel out here.
SHELLEY. What's gonna blow up?
CANDY. Things travel further out here. You know about brain waves. They magnify. They can blow something up like remote control.
SHELLEY. I see. *(They sit quietly for a while; then Shelley gets up and starts to walk toward the car. Candy grabs her and pulls her down.)*
CANDY. Are you crazy?
SHELLEY. It's hot out here.
CANDY. Where are you going? Are you nuts?
SHELLEY. I want my sun visor.
CANDY. Why doesn't anyone ever hear me? Stay. Away. From. The. Car. The car.
SHELLEY. Right. The car. It's a terrific car, Candy. Not a convertible, but—great car.

CANDY. Shelley. I stopped the car — I saved your life in the process by the way — I stopped the car because it was going to blow up. Am I making myself clear? Loud noise? Boom? KA-POWW. Got it?
SHELLEY. Okay. Okay. I got it. That's nuts.
CANDY. The two little red lights on the dash were blinking on and off and there was smoke coming out of the hood and a loud hissing noise like a time bomb.
SHELLEY. Classic paranoia.
CANDY. How do you explain that?
SHELLEY. I thought you were the Radish Festival Goddess from Saints-Preserve-Us Indiana. Am I right, am I right?
CANDY. I am from Indiana, yes.
SHELLEY. Well I was born and raised in New York City and can't drive to save my life but even I know that when a car is overheated steam comes out of the radiator and the little red gizmo light lights up. You must've run into this sort of thing before with your tractor.
CANDY. I don't have to respond to that, thanks.
SHELLEY. Maybe the fertilizer fumes were harmful when you were growing up. They've probably done studies —
CANDY. I have never been within ten feet of a tractor in my life except at the automotive show once a year with my uncle Albert.
SHELLEY. Well you don't have to get so bent out of shape.
CANDY. You think that's all it was?
SHELLEY. Huh?
CANDY. The radiator. Overheated.
SHELLEY. Oh sure. I mean, cars are human too, you know. It must be 110 degrees out here.
CANDY. 113. The radio said.
SHELLEY. I was asleep.
CANDY. And missed another turnoff — Route 452. Where is it?
SHELLEY. Lost in America.
CANDY. Oh, well, that's a relief — it was just overheated. *(Shelley gets up and heads toward the car again; Candy tackles her, grabbing her leg, holding her back.)* Shelley! You'll be killed!
SHELLEY. Will you let go?
CANDY. The hissing noise, the exploding gas tank — they

do that, you know — you haven't explained that part.
SHELLEY. This is really crazy. Hello, leg. (*She shakes herself loose and heads toward the car again.*)
CANDY. Don't leave me.
SHELLEY. I'm gonna fry out here. I'm not used to all this fresh air. Jeez.
CANDY. I'm afraid.
SHELLEY. I'll be right back. (*Shelley gets up and heads for the car; suddenly there is a tremendous boom; Shelley dives behind the rock. Candy and Shelley scream; they cling to each other.*)
CANDY. (*Screams; starts to cry.*) I told you! It blew up! I told you! (*Starts to pummel Shelley.*) You would've killed yourself for a lousy pair of sunglasses.
SHELLEY. My visor blew up, too. I'm gonna melt.
CANDY. And we were always such good friends and I've known you since I moved away from home and we always share everything and understand and I saved your life and now we're just going to die out here.
SHELLEY. And they'll find us years later. Probably some poor innocent little Boy Scouts out on a cookout. And Candy, they'll find our skeletons and they won't even know who we are.
CANDY. Oh no, not some poor little kids. (*Shelley leans back against the rock. Suddenly she flinches and bounces to another part of the rock. She screams.*) What?
SHELLEY. Get it away! What is it? It's killing me! Oh I hate it!
CANDY. Where?
SHELLEY. It's alive. Get it away! Kick it.
CANDY. It's a lizard.
SHELLEY. Tell it to leave. Scat. Shoo!
CANDY. Shelley. One does not tell a lizard to leave. Besides, you get rid of one, 3200 more just show up to replace it. It's an Old Indian custom — Apache, I think.
SHELLEY. (*Gingerly trying to kick the lizard away — and finding it horrible.*) Oh. Oh. I — Candy, he's dead. I murdered it.
CANDY. They shed their skin. It's molting.
SHELLEY. If so, this one got confused and molted everything.
CANDY. Oh.

SHELLEY. Why did I ever let you talk me into t   . trip?
CANDY. You needed a change. I could tell.
SHELLEY. They're killing me. Every rock and rattlesnake and El Rancho Big Boy Breakfast.
CANDY. The open road, Shelley. Think of it.
SHELLEY. They're eating my soul. I'm going to walk out into the desert and let them devour me all at once. (*Shelley starts to walk off, towards the car, out into the desert. Suddenly, she stops.*) That's funny. I must be hallucinating already. The car blew up, but it's still there. It's a mirage. It's like Castaneda or something.
CANDY. Don't go near it! It's . . . it's too weird. (*As if in a trance, Shelley walks offstage to the car; Candy starts to peek over the rock, thinks better of it, and takes cover again. We hear Shelley faintly in the distance—can't quite tell what she is doing. Then:*)
SHELLEY. (*Appearing in view loaded down with their bags and a plastic object.*) HA! Bombs away! (*Shelley tosses the plastic thing over the rock; it lands at Candy's feet.*)
CANDY. (*Scrambling away from it.*) What? Get it away from me. Are you nuts? It's— (*Beat.*) Why, it's an orange juice container.
SHELLEY. (*Entering with a large overstuffed purse or bag and Candy's knapsack.*) Exact-a-men-tay.
CANDY. What a good idea. I'm thirsty.
SHELLEY. Good. Then you won't mind licking orange juice off the luggage.
CANDY. Huh?
SHELLEY. Elementary, my dear Candace. Orange juice—Tuesday. Thrown into backseat. Hot sun. Four days in the car. Desert heat like a laser—zap. Right through rear window. Friday afternoon—that's right now—O.J. ferments and eureka! Explodes! The time bomb, at your service.
CANDY. (*Holding the container as if tickling a baby.*) Oh, so its little self-ums was just letting off steam, wasn't ums?
SHELLEY. Pressure.
CANDY. Like ittle bittle root beer bottles, if you shake em up too much.

SHELLEY. You can't survive without your own bacteria. You can't take a fish out of water.
CANDY. Water. What a good idea. Maybe there's an oasis out there.
SHELLEY. No, there would have to be coconut trees. Gee, a macaroon would be good. I'm starved.
CANDY. If you would have let me buy that ice chest at that K-Mart in Ohio you could eat right now.
SHELLEY. Macaroons don't need an ice chest. Oooh, a cinnamon roll with raisins. Hot from the oven. A steak. Blood red.
CANDY. You're a vegetarian.
SHELLEY. A steak. And nachos. A pepperoncini salad. Onion soup with melted cheese. Fried eggs. A hot pastrami sandwich with sauerkraut. And lasagna. That's what I want. Scratch that. Scratch all of that. Watermelon. Yeah. (*Shelley sighs, then sneezes. Candy hold her arms and legs at weird angles to catch the rays.*)
CANDY. Mm. I know what I want. Yeah. I want hot sex. Hot hot sex.
SHELLEY. In this heat?
CANDY. Hot desert sands, a hot desert breeze, vapors, and a hot hot hot young man.
SHELLEY. (*Sneezing.*) Got any cough syrup?
CANDY. A biker, maybe.
SHELLEY. Even a Kleenex?
CANDY. Biker, mmmm, yeah.
SHELLEY. I need medicine. (*She starts checking pockets, purse, knapsack, for something to take. As she searches, she discovers another mini-corpse.*) No! No! Here's another one! It's a lizard graveyard. What are they doing? What are they doing?
CANDY. One hot hot biker.
SHELLEY. You know, probably if we got in the car and took off, I'd feel a lot better.
CANDY. Or a lot of them. Hubba hubba.
SHELLEY. (*Sneezing; starts packing up their things.*) Well, now that you've had a little rest from driving, we should get going.
CANDY. Yeah. He'd pull up on his hot hot machine. Or they would.

SHELLEY. I promise to follow the map better this time — we'll just drive uptown until we hit I-80, then turn right. That's east, got it? Uh, like taking the FDR up to the 59th Street Bridge. See?
CANDY. Ooooh. Bikers like those guys with the shrunken heads on their helmets that we saw at that last Foster's Freeze. Oooooo-eee Vrrummm, rrummm. Rummmm. (*She sits up, grasps "handlebars" and "kicks the bike into gear" — as if she were really on a chopper.*)
SHELLEY. Uh, Candy, catch my drift there? Like, we'll go home.
CANDY. You wanted to see the Pacific Ocean. Rrrummmm, RRRRummm.
SHELLEY. I'm sure it looks just like the Atlantic. Just the same except it's on the wrong side when you look at it.
CANDY. Never saw a biker eat a vanilla cone with sprinkles before.
SHELLEY. Candy. Look. It's about time we admitted that this so-called get-away-from-it-all experience is not working out.
CANDY. All those sprinkles, he kind of closed his eyes and . . . oh.
SHELLEY. Maybe the Bahamas this fall — a nice condo on the water, I think.
CANDY. Mmm. And then that one teeny drip of icy . . . white . . . frozen . . . custard . . . cream, just one drip on his chest, kind of melting down over his —
SHELLY. Candy, let's go.
CANDY. Mmm. He had a real good tan and a lot of terrific blonde hair on his chest, did you notice that?
SHELLEY. Yeah, but he was peeling. Let's go. We've gotta get somewhere civilized before dark.
CANDY. I'd lick it off.
SHELLEY. (*Sneezing.*) I'm sick.
CANDY. Come on, think of it. A steamy biker boy. Spikes on his cap. Thighs all swathed in leather.
SHELLEY. In this heat?
CANDY. Relax. They've got us where they want us. We're at their mercy now. They're just waiting till we get a little

weaker, then they'll swoop in for the kill. (*Beat.*) Hear their bikes. Rrrummm, rrrummm.
SHELLEY. Please. We've had enough. I'll be good. I swear it. I'm sorry I made you stop at that Union 76 trucker place in Iowa. I know you didn't want to.
CANDY. Oooh. I am ready for you, Mr. Desert Man.
SHELLEY. (*Trying to drag Candy to the car.*) You've got to take me home now.
CANDY. (*Singing the Little Eva song.*) Chains! My baby's got me locked up in chains . . . and it ain't the kind . . . that you can see . . .
SHELLEY. So . . . here's the plan. I'll go to the car. I'll get in and sit down and you'll come over there in a second or two and we'll drive off. Simple. I'm sorry you have to drive all the way. I'll . . . I'll pay for all the motels going back. Okay? Look, it's just that I never learned to drive stick shift, that's all. Hey . . . we'll drive along and I'll really learn this time. You work the pedals, and I'll shift. Right? (*Candy continues humming the song, while deliberately and sensuously basking in the sun.*) Candy. Listen to me. This is the kind of place where lunatics bury hundreds of sunburned tourists in the sand after they chop them into little pieces and set fire to their baby oil. People carry axes out here.
CANDY. Mmmmm, motor boy.
SHELLEY. Candy, cut it out. Now look —
CANDY. Ohh ohh take me.
SHELLEY. Candy — (*Candy continues humming, then stops abruptly. There are sounds of bikers off in the distance.*) Oh God.
CANDY. Wow.
SHELLEY. Snap out of it. This is serious now.
CANDY. Wow I didn't really think they would really —
SHELLEY. We've gotta get out of here. (*The sounds of the motorcycles grow louder and louder.*)
CANDY. Wow. Dozens of little specks, all heading this way.
SHELLEY. Oh no.
CANDY. Gee. And there's more behind them.
SHELLEY. Candy!
CANDY. Wow. Like an ant farm. (*Shelley's anxiety is escalating — in fact, she's in a full-scale panic.*)

SHELLEY. Hurry! LOOK! (*Shelley points Candy in the direction of the approaching bikers.*) What do I have to do to get you to move?
CANDY. Oh God no! (*Candy, who has been intransigent, finally realizes the danger — then runs.*)
SHELLEY. Come on!
CANDY. (*Stops abruptly.*) Wait. I'll go.
SHELLEY. Candy!
CANDY. But there's just one thing I want.
SHELLEY. Tell me. Fast!
CANDY. Did you sleep with Roger?
SHELLEY. What?
CANDY. Tell me.
SHELLEY. Candy.
CANDY. They're coming. They're almost here. I can smell them.
SHELLEY. (*Beat.*) Yes. I did.
CANDY. Aha!
SHELLEY. But you had already stopped seeing him.
CANDY. Some friend.
SHELLEY. Please, Candy, can't we just discuss this at some nice safe Hojo's in Nebraska? Come on, the little specks on the horizon are turning into nasty growly men on big dirty machines.
CANDY. So you did.
SHELLEY. We'll be murdered. Raped.
CANDY. Doesn't matter now.
SHELLEY. (*The bikers are practically on top of them now.*) I'm too young to die.
CANDY. Maybe I'll just walk off into the des— (*Shelley tackles Candy and pushes her behind the rock, out of view.*)
SHELLEY. I'm too old for this. (*The biker sounds swell and peak, then the bikers pass. Motorcycle engines finally begin to fade in the distance. Shelley peeks up over the top of the rock—we see only her head. She sneezes.*) All clear. (*Shelley climbs on top of the rock.*) Candy? Hey! You can come out now! (*Candy does not respond. Shelley tries not to notice. Looking off in the distance:*) Hey, Candy, wow. Look. It's some kind of furry animal or— it's moving! It's moving! Oh, look at him go! You don't like

those silly bikers either, do ya, pal? You said it, fella, buncha noise and hot air, that's all they are. (*Without Shelley noticing, Candy stands up on the other side of the rock, turns, and begins to walk off into the desert.*) You know, Can, you're right about tan lines. Who needs em? (*She takes off her sandals, tosses them aside. Something is stuck to one of them: another lizard stiff. She picks up the body.*) You guys, you guys, this is really starting to break my heart now. Is this some kind of trans-species death wish or what? Oh, what can I do for you little awful things? (*As Shelley talks, she gingerly gathers up the lizard bodies and arranges them, somewhat reverently, on a ledge of the rock. She makes a little design out of them — lizards all in a circle, a pentagram, or what-ever — and then makes a marker for the "grave" out of pebbles or even one of her earrings. Working on the lizards:*) Hey Can? You should've had a hat on in this heat. People never go to the desert without a hat. No wonder you got so upset. Over Roger. My God. What a waste. (*Beat.*) I'll lend you my sunglasses. That'll be good. (*To a lizard.*) Look at you. Where'd you lose your little foot? You like this place? (*Smelling the lotion on her hands; to Candy.*) This is nice suntan lotion. Mmm. Smells like almonds. There's a poison that smells like almonds — what is it? Arsenic? Maybe strychnine. They always mention that in my Agatha Christie's. So I always know when someone mentions almonds there's some clue. (*Finishing with the lizards.*) There. That's nice. Maybe you won't be lizards next time. Maybe you'll come back as mountain lions or wild horses or, who knows? You could have your own talk show. Now the rest of you guys out there, stay well. (*She settles back down on the rock; she takes in the desert, the sky, the limitless space.*) Candy. Come out come out wherever you are. Can. Come on now. This trip is not going to be any fun if you don't talk to me. (*Shelley goes to the other side of the rock. Candy is not there.*) Oh no. Oh no oh no oh no oh no. Candy! Candy! (*Shelley looks for Candy, but doesn't see her anywhere. Shelley heads off into the desert, disappearing offstage.*) Candy! (*She calls for Candy offstage — growing further away.*) Candy! (*In a moment we hear a rustling sound. Shelley appears, dragging a half-conscious Candy. Shelley props her up under the rock. She fans her with her visor — or a PEOPLE Magazine. She*

s a small shelter—out of an umbrella from her bag, or a etched out towel—for shade.) Candy. Speak to me. Say something.
CANDY. Where am I?
SHELLEY. Oh hell.
CANDY. I must've passed out or something.
SHELLEY. Something.
CANDY. You saved my life.
SHELLEY. That's ridiculous.
CANDY. Well, you did. (*Beat.*) I'll never forget it.
SHELLEY. Why? Just tell me why? Why did you go off in this sun? Not because of Roger. Couldn't be. That's too stupid.
CANDY. Roger? Now I remember. I'll never speak to you again.
SHELLEY. Oh come on. (*No response.*) We're best friends. (*No response.*) It wasn't my idea. It was his. I mean, it just happened, there was a certain thing, a certain feeling.
CANDY. Oh. A feeling.
SHELLEY. It happened and then it passed. (*No response.*) You hadn't seen him in a month. (*No response.*) Besides, you always told me he had funny feet and you didn't like the way he said "howdy boys and girls" all the time. Candy, I saved your life.
CANDY. I saved yours, too. From the bomb that was orange juice. So we're even. Fuck you.
SHELLEY. Look, I wouldn't ever want to do anything to hurt you, or hurt your feelings, you're the one I want to help through the hurt, not hurt, I mean, there's hurt out there and we can be hurt, know what I mean?
CANDY. No. Do you?
SHELLEY. I'm your friend. Why didn't you tell me how you were feeling—
CANDY. Cause everyone knows that a friend is the one person you don't have to tell cause they know how you feel and you're supposed to know that, so there.
SHELLEY. I didn't know you cared about him. You said you didn't. (*Beat.*) I should've known you were just saying it. (*Beat.*) I'm the lowliest homeliest pebble. I'm the stones under your shoes. I should be shot. Can. Can, I could make it up to you. I could. (*Beat.*) You know, nobody. Nobody cares

for me the way you do. Nobody. Tout le monde. (*Beat.*) I really want to thank you for this trip.
CANDY. Oh stop being so patronizing.
SHELLEY. No. Really. Sitting on that rock a minute ago, I had a feeling—
CANDY. Oh, a feeling. How nice. The same feeling you got when you screwed Roger?
SHELLEY. I'm serious. You know I am. In the city—you know this—in the city I work day and night just to keep food in the catbowls. Day in. Day out. Winter. Summer. I'm either gasping for breath when what's left of our oxygen is frozen, or I'm gagging on hot wet smells, smothering in still air, everything stuck like glue. The city is psychic Bombay. Last week, last week, Sylvia at work gives me a new mug with rabbits on it. Immediately I fill it with caffeine and wire myself to the ceiling. I spend my days up there. Nights, I go home from work, make some awful dinner—either junk food or stuff from the health food store, it all tastes the same. Then I call you. That's the best part of the day. I force myself to do the dishes first, so that after I call you I don't have anything awful to do anymore. One night, I call you and you say, let's go to the desert. Let's go have a lot of space, a lot of air, a lot of room to be free. And I'm standing by my window and all of a sudden, it happens. The veil is lifted. There's a slight breeze, the buildings all carved out of light. I realize why I'm here. I can move again. So I say, yes, let's go. Let's. And we do. And I climb up on this rock and start to see a lot of things. And then you—you get mad. You take it all away. I guess I understand why. But I never thought I was doing anything wrong. So I'm sorry. (*Beat.*) Things'll be different now, huh? Yeah. (*Beat.*) It really didn't mean anything, Can. It just happened.
CANDY. Is that supposed to be some kind of confession? Pretty feeble.
SHELLEY. No. It's just that this is today. Today is us. Right here, right now, you and me. (*Beat.*) Oh God, what am I saying? (*Beat.*) So. When did you find out? Right after it happened? Last week when we decided to come out here? Did you figure we'd be trapped in a car for oh so many thousand miles and we could confront each other? (*Beat.*)

Roger told you, didn't he? That scum.
CANDY. It wasn't Roger.
SHELLEY. You're just protecting him.
CANDY. So?
SHELLEY. So? So you fell for him, he didn't fall for you, he used you, he left you, you deserve better, and he's not even good in bed.
CANDY. Maybe not the first time. Maybe not for one time, but for—forget it. I don't want you telling me how many times. I don't want details.
SHELLEY. So there are other men, worthy of your loyalty and protection.
CANDY. I loved Roger. I felt close to him. He was special.
SHELLEY. I'm your friend.
CANDY. So?
SHELLEY. So why don't you protect me?
CANDY. I have. Go away. It's different anyway. Him and me. You and me. It's not the same thing at all.
SHELLEY. Yeah. You're right.
CANDY. Besides. You are now not my friend.
SHELLEY. No. Maybe not. (*Shelley stands on top of the rock.*) Oh, I feel like I'm way out there. Out beyond where we can see. That's where I think I am. I have more of a real connection with myself being way out on the vanishing point than I do with myself being here. (*Beat.*) This was your idea. I won't ever be the same again. I think I could even drive the car. I bet I could. Funny. I guess we'll go back now, which is a shame because finally, finally I could almost see going on. Driving right up to the edge of the Pacific. Now I don't suppose we'll do that.
CANDY. No. You spoiled it.
SHELLEY. Right. I forgot.
CANDY. It's just as well. I'm better off now. Everything is more clearly defined. Now that I don't have to answer to you anymore I can do anything I want. Maybe be a torch singer in a nightclub. Maybe find a husband and grow peanuts. Who knows?
SHELLEY. I don't know.
CANDY. Well, whatever. It will be exciting. That's all I know.

SHELLEY. That's good. I want it to be exciting.
CANDY. I don't have to be famous. I'll settle for a cult following.
SHELLEY. Oh, don't settle for anything but the best.
CANDY. I was being serious.
SHELLEY. Sorry.
CANDY. I was thinking of hopes. You wouldn't know anything about that. Last week I called you—
SHELLEY. Yes—
CANDY. And we decided we could get away from it all 'cause it would all be there when we got back, only better.
SHELLEY. Yes.
CANDY. And then I ran into Roger. And he was in love.
SHELLEY. Oh?
CANDY. With you.
SHELLEY. No he isn't.
CANDY. I don't want to talk about it.
SHELLEY. He isn't. He can't be. I haven't even talked to him in over three months.
CANDY. Who needs to talk?
SHELLEY. Oh stop it.
CANDY. We'll go now. It'll be getting dark. (*Lights begin a very slow change, from now to end of play, lighting the stage first with various and varying shades of lurid sunset colors—the kind you only see in the west.*)
SHELLEY. Okay. Wait. This feels terrible, this between us. What can I do? I'll do anything to fix it and make it better.
CANDY. Who can trust you?
SHELLEY. Please. Candy. Really. Anything. Name something.
CANDY. Tell him you never want to see him again.
SHELLEY. Yes, of course.
CANDY. Nah. Too easy. Tell him I'm the one who left the Rilke sonnets on his doorstep, not you.
SHELLEY. Rilke sonnets? Yeah. Sure.
CANDY. No. It was dumb of me. Let him think you're the sap. Tell him you're marrying some guy from your hometown.
SHELLEY. New York is my hometown.
CANDY. What do you say?

SHELLEY. Fine. Okay. Only don't let me ruin your life.
CANDY. No. No, you least of all should ruin it.
SHELLEY. That's right. There are other, far more worthy opponents.
CANDY. Aha. So you are an opponent then?
SHELLEY. No! Oh no! Just a figure of speech. No, I just mean save your strength for a truly dangerous—
CANDY. As if you aren't.
SHELLEY. Now don't start.
CANDY. So we'll go.
SHELLEY. Yes. Absolutely. And we are friends. You said so.
CANDY. Not yet. Maybe in Wyoming.
SHELLEY. So you don't hate me. (*Candy starts to gather up their things.*)
CANDY. Maybe. I don't know. (*As Candy stuffs magazines, sunscreen, etc. into the bags, a biker, in mirrored sunglasses, black leather, and a helmet, appears in the distance. He has a hand raised in front of him — but the way he's moving, it's hard to tell if it's a greeting, a threat, or a basic ward-off position.*)
SHELLEY. Oh God. (*Grabbing Candy.*) When I say go, get into the car. We'll run him over.
RON (THE BIKER). Hey—
SHELLEY. Get back! I'm warning you. I'll throw this. (*Shelley throws the orange juice container; it hits the biker on the head, catching him off guard, and he loses his balance and falls.*)
CANDY. You've killed him. (*The biker gets back up.*) Throw it again.
SHELLEY. Get back!
CANDY. There's two of us. We'll hurt you. Oh, Mary, mother of—
SHELLEY. Let's go! (*They start to run off into the desert — but where? Toward what?*)
CANDY. Where do we— (*The biker comes closer. They are trapped.*) Oh boy—
SHELLEY. Do you want us to put our hands up or something? (*Candy, still covered in globs of sunscreen, and Shelley in visor and mirrored lenses, put their hands up. The biker immediately raises his arms, too, as if to attack. Shelley lowers, then raises, her hands.*) We'll just keep our hands up here so you'll know

that we're scared, I mean, peaceful. Uh, me Shelley, me peaceloving.
CANDY. Sshh. He's not an Indian. He's a — oh God — biker. Jesus. (*Ron the biker doesn't respond. He picks up both their purses, plus the orange juice container. Basically, he is as wary of them as vice versa. He thinks they might be crazy — or at the very least, dangerous.*)
SHELLEY. See, if we would've left when I wanted to.
RON (THE BIKER). Uh. Shut up. Both of you, away from there. Move, move. (*Ron goes through their things, searching for something.*)
SHELLEY. You can have all our money. Uh, sorry there isn't much.
CANDY. It's all in traveler's checks. We could make them all out to you.
SHELLEY. Don't be silly. Bikers don't have bank accounts.
CANDY. So?
SHELLEY. So how would he cash them?
CANDY. Why, we could go with him.
SHELLEY. What a good idea! Why don't we all drive to the bank?
RON (THE BIKER). What?
SHELLEY. We could get the money in quarters — you could play the slots. Double it in an afternoon.
RON (THE BIKER). Shut up. (*Ron, a little woozy from the heat and from Shelley's blow on the head, checks all the linings of their things, looking for something dangerous. As Shelley comes closer to him, he holds her off, threatening her with the orange juice container.*)
SHELLEY. It was only a suggestion.
CANDY. Shut up.
RON (THE BIKER). All right — what do you have? Knives? A shotgun maybe?
CANDY. Huh?
SHELLEY. If my memory serves me, this is the man of your dreams.
CANDY. Stop it. (*To Ron.*) Oh, not you. Her. Uh, you do what you want. I mean — oh God. That's not what I mean. Uh . . .
SHELLEY. That's right. Gang up on me.

RON (THE BIKER). You two are strange.
SHELLEY. True.
RON (THE BIKER). You know, you two should be careful. You could hurt somebody.
CANDY. Huh? Oh. That. We weren't really going to run you over.
SHELLEY. Nah. The car won't even start.
RON (THE BIKER). *(Holding up the juice container.)* How do you explain this?
SHELLEY. It's just orange juice. Maybe you were thirsty. I just have bad aim.
RON (THE BIKER). I don't know what to do with you two. *(Ron is sweltering; he tries to pull off his leathers, but the zipper is stuck. Note: For Ron's costume, a one-piece leather biking suit is a possibility, or, a leather jacket with matching black pants. The important point is, he is trapped in the outfit in the heat.)* Damn zipper. Heat'll kill me. *(As Candy moves toward him.)* Stay away from me.
CANDY. Sorry. I was just trying to get into the shade.
RON (THE BIKER). There isn't any and you know it. Not for hundreds of miles.
CANDY. I see what you mean. *(Ron, slightly dizzy, leans against the rock. He then sees Shelley's lizard graves.)*
RON (THE BIKER). So . . . what? Are you some weird cult or something? You collecting this nutsy stuff out here to cast some kind of crazy spell? Or — poison?
SHELLEY. Poison? Like almonds? Hey do you read Ag —
CANDY. Shut up.
RON (THE BIKER). So. That's it.
CANDY. No. We're just a coupla regular kinda gals.
RON (THE BIKER). Sure. Sure you are. Look. I need some gasoline — hey, get back.
SHELLEY. We passed a station about twenty miles back. Chevron. I could give you my credit card. Just head that way.
RON (THE BIKER). Don't get cute.
SHELLEY. Just trying to be helpful.
RON (THE BIKER). You got a gas can or anything? *(They shake their heads, no.)* Something wrong with your wheels? What? You on empty? *(Candy is totally tongue-tied; when she does try to speak, no sound comes out.)*

SHELLEY. Radiator.
RON (THE BIKER). Gee. Too bad. There isn't any water out here.
SHELLEY. So we noticed.
RON (THE BIKER). Hey. I'm sorry you're having problems — whoa, keep over there. But, uh, listen. I've got a siphon, and I'm, uh, just gonna help myself to a little gasoline — I only need a gallon. Uh, here's a couple bucks, that should cover it. Wait. I'll put the money on the rock. And, I'll send a tow truck out to get you once I've gotten a head start.
SHELLEY. A head start? You running from the law or something?
RON (THE BIKER). No. Are you?
SHELLEY. Don't be silly.
RON (THE BIKER). Are you sure?
CANDY. Oh, come on — do we look like —
RON (THE BIKER). Uh . . . uh . . . get your hands up. Stay back. Now, uh, listen ladies, this has been very interesting, meeting you out here in the middle of nowhere and all, but I've got to get going and I don't want any trouble, so just keep away while I get the gas, it'll just take a minute, I'm gonna freckle if I don't get outa this sun pretty soon.
CANDY. What're you gonna put the gasoline in?
RON (THE BIKER). *(Holds out juice container.)* This.
CANDY. But that's our bomb.
SHELLEY. Ssshhh.
RON (THE BIKER). Oh man, have I got to get out of here. *(Ron starts toward the car.)*
CANDY. Do you have any of those shrunken heads?
RON (THE BIKER). What?
CANDY. Shelley, ask him where you get those heads.
RON (THE BIKER). Are you talking to me? Look. I'll just take a minute. Then you can go back to whatever weird ceremony is going on out here. Just forget you ever saw me. *(Ron exits.)*
SHELLEY. Ooh. Motor man. He's really here.
CANDY. Stop making fun of me. See, I should never think things. The abstract always gets me into some kind of trouble in the concrete. *(Ron reappears.)*

SHELLEY. So. Do you have your gasoline?
RON (THE BIKER). No. There's a hole in the jug.
CANDY. Yeah. We blew it up.
RON (THE BIKER). (*Staggers; the heat is getting to him.*) Look. I don't know who you two are, or what you're up to, but I'm getting sunstroke. Now I want to just lie down for a moment, under this rock, and please, just leave me be and don't turn me into a lizard or anything. (*Ron sits at the edge of the rock, takes a goatskin bag from inside his clothes, and drinks.*)
SHELLEY. Wow. What's that?
CANDY. Can we have some?
RON (THE BIKER). I'll . . . I'll hold it while you drink. You can have more when I wake up. Don't try to take it while I'm asleep, or—well, something. (*Ron gives them each a drink.*)
CANDY. I can't place it.
SHELLEY. Southern Comfort. No, Sangria.
CANDY. (*Finally identifying the drink.*) Kool-aid!! (*Ron eyes them suspiciously, arranges the goatskin under him, and settles into sleep.*)
SHELLEY. Comfortable?
RON (THE BIKER). Please . . . leave me alone.
CANDY. Maybe he could use our pillow?
SHELLEY. It's plastic—he wouldn't want that.
CANDY. I could cover it. (*Candy cautiously approaches the stretched out Ron.*) I think he's asleep.
SHELLEY. Already?
CANDY. Must be tired from all that biking—those machines must weigh a ton.
SHELLEY. Candy, he balances the thing, he doesn't carry it.
CANDY. Still. (*Beat.*) He's got nice eyelashes.
SHELLEY. They're okay. I wonder why he doesn't shave his head.
CANDY. Or wear it real long.
SHELLEY. Must be the latest thing.
CANDY. We should make some shade.
SHELLEY. Yeah. (*Candy reaches for a towel with which to shade Ron. Shelley, having nothing else, removes her blouse, sits on the rock over Ron, and makes a canopy, spreading the blouse over her legs. She is wearing a halter top—perfect for an ice cream stand on*

the boardwalk. Candy joins her on the rock, draping the towel over her legs.) Now what?
CANDY. Now we wait.
SHELLEY. I guess. *(They are silent a moment. The silence is very strange. The light continues changing, casting odd shadows.)*
CANDY. Jesus.
SHELLEY. Yeah.
CANDY. Hey! We could play cards!
SHELLEY. Oh. Good idea. Do we have any?
CANDY. I got a deck with my car insurance. Free.
SHELLEY. Great.
CANDY. I think I left them at home.
SHELLEY. *(Beat.)* Are you sleepy? We should nap, maybe. Conserve your strength. Go ahead. You sleep. I'll keep watch.
CANDY. Watch what? *(Candy puts her hands to her face, using them like binoculars, trying to isolate a patch of desert in the distance.)* What's that?
SHELLEY. Where?
CANDY. See. Straight ahead. In line with my finger.
SHELLEY. A cactus.
CANDY. Yeah. What does that look like to you?
SHELLEY. Uh. Green. Well, I wouldn't say GREEN green. More like a dusky green. Greyish. Spikes — no, fuzz. Brown at sides — looks broken.
CANDY. Uh-huh. *(Looking at it.)* It doesn't look like a seal in a circus balancing a ball to you?
SHELLEY. Well, I don't know, maybe if I squint.
CANDY. Now I've got circus music in my head.
SHELLEY. Candy! Relax.
CANDY. I don't see what's there, I see whatever I think. And I can't stop thinking.
SHELLEY. Think of something deserty then. Imagine you're right here.
CANDY. My brain can change anything on the whole lousy planet into absolutely anything else — except for one tiny detail.
SHELLEY. What?
CANDY. Me.
SHELLEY. Uh, Can, that's fortunate, don't you think? I

mean, suppose you thought "bumblebee" and off you flew.
CANDY. I don't know. (*Beat.*) To me, the ultimate most incredible thing would be to simply disappear in a puff of smoke and emerge as someone else — someone I'd want to become this time around. You think that's religious, maybe?
SHELLEY. Sure. Maybe.
CANDY. Someone amazing. In control.
SHELLEY. Yeah. (*As they talk, the twilight becomes even more vivid. Ron lies there, eyes open, but resting, lulled, watching and listening, under his canopy.*)
CANDY. Madame de Pompadour.
SHELLEY. Not her.
CANDY. Freud?
SHELLEY. Unh-unh.
CANDY. Scarlett O'Hara.
SHELLEY. She didn't exist.
CANDY. Scarlett O'Hara. Before the Civil War, when she was a young southern belle, when she walked into a room everyone else faded to grey. That's all. And then, when the war was over — you know that scene — when everything was destroyed and no one was left, the land was naked earth, and everything was dead. She didn't give up. She crawled, she scrambled all over that muddy field until she found an old gnarly turnip or carrot or some damned thing with clumps of black dirt all over it and she picked it up and ate the whole damned mud-covered rutabaga, because no one was going to put her down. She was going to survive. And she made a dress out of drapes from the front parlor window and took on the whole Union army and Clark Gable, too, stronger than ever, because she was somebody, somebody who always got what she wanted. Who everybody admired. (*Beat.*) Oh. No. I couldn't be her anyway.
SHELLEY. She didn't exist.
CANDY. I'd get sick if I ate the damned dirty potato and I'd look like hell in window drapes.
SHELLEY. Well, you'd do it if you had to. You and me — we could handle anything.
CANDY. No, I don't think so.
SHELLEY. Come on, we can handle anything.
CANDY. Nope. Not me. This is you we're talking about.

SHELLEY. Oh. I guess. Well, sometimes.
CANDY. Yeah. You can.
SHELLEY. Really. (*Beat.*) That's not who I am.
CANDY. Oh. (*Beat.*) No?
SHELLEY. No.
CANDY. (*Beat.*) Yeah. I know.
SHELLEY. You don't want to be Scarlett O'Hara.
CANDY. No.
SHELLEY. Probably wasn't happy anyway. Candy. There is some reason why we came from who we were then to be here. To where we are going.
CANDY. Yes. I can see the distance we've traveled.
SHELLEY. Yeah. Oh feel it out here. (*Appreciating this.*) A person's really alone out here.
RON (THE BIKER). Wow. The desert is really getting crazy.
CANDY. Hey! I thought you were asleep.
RON (THE BIKER). I'm gonna start spending my vacations in Minnesota from now on.
CANDY. You're an eavesdropper, aren't you? That's rude.
RON (THE BIKER). Sorry. There didn't seem to be anyplace to go at the moment.
SHELLEY. (*Pulling her blouse back on.*) You're an eyedropper, too.
RON (THE BIKER). You guys are okay, you know that? I liked hearing you. Like music that makes you feel good. You know, not supermarket stuff. (*Ron gets up, tugs at the zipper of his leathers again.*) Excuse me, I've got to get out of this. (*He tries to free the zipper, but it won't budge. Candy and Shelley approach tentatively, then try to help him pull off the jacket without undoing the zipper. It's a tug-of-war; they end up on the ground but the jacket finally comes off and Ron is free. He then also removes his outer leather pants. Underneath the leather he has on a midwestern-looking pair of shorts, somewhat baggy, and a corny T-shirt.*)
CANDY. Say. What are you?
RON (THE BIKER). Huh? You mean my sign?
CANDY. You're no biker.
RON (THE BIKER). Sure I am.
CANDY. Oh yeah. Hell's Angel? Born to be wild?

RON (THE BIKER). Uh, well, no. (*Beat.*) Hi. My name's Ron.
CANDY. This guy is a fake.
RON (THE BIKER). Look, I've got a nice little Honda — fixed her up myself. Drove her all the way out from Michigan.
SHELLEY. I'll bet.
RON (THE BIKER). Ypsilanti.
CANDY. Nothing is exciting anymore. There is no romance left in life.
RON (THE BIKER). Gee. That makes me feel sad.
SHELLEY. Sometimes it's hard to be a woman.
CANDY. That's for sure.
RON (THE BIKER). Is it?
CANDY. Yeah.
RON (THE BIKER). Gee I would've thought — well, gee. Well. Wow. (*Beat.*) Hard to be a biker, too. Hard to be a man. Life's too crazy. I get lost.
SHELLEY. Our map has orange juice on it.
RON (THE BIKER). Yeah. I know what you mean.
SHELLEY. I just meant the map got wet.
CANDY. Ah, who needs bikers anyway.
RON (THE BIKER). Thanks loads.
CANDY. (*Climbs up on the rock.*) I wonder how far we'd have to walk to get to the Interstate. (*The sunset is approaching its most vivid now — orange, fuchsia, magenta — radiating.*)
RON (THE BIKER). The Interstate? I-80? Yeah, that's where I was headed, too.
CANDY. Great.
SHELLEY. Well, you know what they say. All roads lead to Rome.
RON (THE BIKER). Nah, I was going to my cousin's wedding. In Livermore. My mother's gonna kill me if I'm late. It's a straight shot, you know. Pick up 80 outside of Toledo, then head straight on out to San Francisco. You ever been there?
SHELLEY. Huh? No. Never been there. Never've been anywhere. Till now, I guess.
RON (THE BIKER). The Bay is navy blue.

CANDY. Hey. Come up here. Come and look.
RON (THE BIKER). Guess I should've stayed on I-80. But I wanted to check out the mountains. There was actually snow up top — one place, anyway. I got pretty cold — the wind was coming up. But clean. And clear — Started winding down the mountain to get back on track. And I ran outa gas.
SHELLEY. And there's a hole in the jug. Funny what can stick you, huh? Here we are. All three. Stuck.
CANDY. Sshh. Look. God, look. Come on. Both of you. Shelley. Come on. Look.
RON (THE BIKER). Gee. And I was supposed to give her away. My first time.
CANDY. Look. (*Shelley and Ron climb up on the rock.*)
SHELLEY. Careful you don't mess up my design.
RON (THE BIKER). Well move your lizards then — they're —
CANDY. Sshh. Come on. Just be quiet. We have to return to a former feeling. A really good feeling.
SHELLEY. Does this mean we'll all three have sex?
RON (THE BIKER). Uh, gee, guys, I uh . . . I don't think I'm ready for this.
CANDY. Shelley, stop playing around.
SHELLEY. (*Beat.*) I *was* getting somewhere before.
CANDY. Try it again.
SHELLEY. Oh wow. I mean, serious wow. (*Taking the desert in.*) Candy, feel that. Ron, you too. (*Beat.*) You know, Can. I don't think I ever made it with Roger. I'm sure I fell asleep.
CANDY. Sshh.
SHELLEY. Yeah. Oh yeah. I'm getting filled up. Candy, it's great, huh? Ron. Try it. Come on. We've got a lot of stuff ahead of us. We need to take something away with us from here.
RON (THE BIKER). Are we doing a spell?
SHELLEY. Sure. If you insist. (*There is a long full moment, as the three of them bask in the wildly colored glow of the desert sunset.*) Reality. Who'd believe it?
CANDY. Mmm.
SHELLEY. (*Beat.*) Ron, you got anymore of that Kool-aid?
RON (THE BIKER). Huh. Sure. (*Transfixed by the desert*

colors, Ron hands Shelley the goatskin. She drinks, then passes it to Candy. Ron and Shelley stare into the distance. Candy takes a drink—stops.)
CANDY. Shelley! Shelley!
SHELLEY. What? What?
CANDY. The car might like some Kool-aid.
SHELLEY. Sure. Cars are human, too, you know.
CANDY. Grape Kool-aid—
RON (THE BIKER). Black cherry.
CANDY. Black cherry Kool-aid into the radiator, and then we could drive Ron to his bike and we could siphon some of our gas right into his tank—
SHELLEY. I don't know, the radiator's bigger than that.
CANDY. We've got a flat Pepsi with a bug in it. Two-liter disposable bottle. We can use that too.
SHELLEY. Pepsi is really bad for you, you shouldn't drink it.
CANDY. The car! Come on. *(Candy climbs down from the rock and gathers up all their gear.)* This is the old pioneer spirit, you know, the settlers all pitching in together to raise the barn, to save the wheat crop. You've seen the movies. America, America. *(Candy exits toward the car with their bags.)*
RON (THE BIKER). Yeah. Yeah, okay. Just a moment. I'm almost getting the feeling.
CANDY. *(Calling from offstage.)* Shelley!
SHELLEY. He's getting the feeling.
CANDY. *(Off.)* It's a nice bonus. Help me with the radiator.
SHELLEY. Okay. *(Shelley doesn't move. She continues to stare off into the desert. We become aware that she is staring off where Ron also is looking. They are aware of each other. They move closer together, without looking at each other.)*
CANDY. *(Off.)* Hi, Happy Mr. Radiator Cap. There you go. Don't like grape? Oh sure you do. It's black cherry anyway. And some cola. Num num.
RON (THE BIKER). I feel like I'm growing bigger. Taller. Fuller.
CANDY. *(Off.)* Shelley! Ron! Come on, Ron. We're saving you, too.
RON (THE BIKER). I am. I'm sure of it.

SHELLEY. Hi Ron.
RON (THE BIKER). Hi Shelley. (*Beat.*) Nice. (*Candy reenters and her triumph over the car is instantly deflated when she sees Shelley and Ron transfixed, quiet, lost in a moment — together. Upset, Candy heads back toward the car. Then she stops herself. Defiantly, she heads back to the rock.*)
CANDY. Shelley.
SHELLEY. Huh? Wow. We have all just drunk from the fountain of life.
CANDY. The car.
SHELLEY. Car? Oh. Great. That's great. I — great. (*She rouses herself and climbs down off the rock.*) Well. Shall we get on with it? Whatever happens? (*Candy just glares at her.*) Ron, come on. Not too much now — there'll be plenty more later.
RON (THE BIKER). Yeah. (*Ron slowly tears himself away from the desert — and the moment with Shelley — and climbs off the rock. He begins to gather his things, then gazing out at the desert one last time, exits to the car. Shelley starts to follow.*)
CANDY. Shelley.
SHELLEY. Yeah?
CANDY. I have the keys.
SHELLEY. Huh?
CANDY. So . . . *not* whatever happens.
SHELLEY. Oh. Oh that. Just watching the sunset. (*Candy doesn't respond.*) Honest, Can. So . . . let's go, huh? (*Candy ignores her.*) Hey. Ready? (*Giving up, Shelley leaves. Candy looks off into the desert, taking in the sky, gazing off at the point that captured Ron and Shelley. The sky is fading to deep purple. A few edges of the rock catch the last glaring rays of the sun. The lizard graveyard almost seems to glow, almost radioactive. Candy crosses to the lizards. She picks one up, closes her eyes, kisses the lizard on the lips, and waits. It does not turn into a prince. She picks up another lizard, kisses it. Nothing. She kisses another and another. Shelley calls from offstage.*) Candy! (*Candy tosses the last lizard over her shoulder and heads toward the car. Sound of the car pulling off, heading down the highway. We hear music from the radio, then a voice. Radio DJ: Yeah. That's how to play it. That one was for all you long distance truckers out there, traveling the coyote trail. And this next one . . . this one's for the ladies . . . The*

trail. And this next one . . . this one's for the ladies . . . The next song . . . say, "Mr. Sandman" or "Born to Be Wild"* . . . plays over the radio, as the desert sky fades to the first blue of night.)

END

Special Note Alternative Disc Jockey Pre-show and Post-show Material: Country and western song plays. Music ends, and The Mickey and Conroy Show broadcast from downtown Winnemucca, Nevada, continues sending its message out to the more desolate stretches of I-80:

MICKEY. What a way to end a Friday afternoon, with (Name of country and western song).
CONROY. Damn it if I didn't have a dog sung like that.
MICKEY. This is Mickey Miller . . .
CONROY. . . . And Conroy Bates . . .
MICKEY. And that cooling trend is holding up nicely, Conroy.
CONROY. Yes sir, all those of you on the road, it's a sweet 113 in the shade.
MICKEY. Boy are we gonna have us one wild weekend!
CONROY. Yes sir!
MICKEY. Yes sir!
CONROY. (*Abruptly perplexed.*) We are?
MICKEY. Yes we are, Conroy.
CONROY. I *was* gonna cart that load of tire rims over to the dump.
MICKEY. That's right, you're busy. But I'm gonna see all you listeners down at J.J.'s Feed and Video Rental for that Charlene Tilton lookalike contest.
CONROY. You are?
MICKEY. Too bad you're booked. And tomorrow mornin' we got the Volunteer Firemen's Donut-Fry. And let's not forget Saturday night at the Rustler's Club. We got wet T-shirt night, boys and girls!
CONROY. We do?

---

*See Special Note on copyright page.

MICKEY. Lookin' forward to judgin' that one.
CONROY. I could change my plans.
MICKEY. Already got two judges, Conroy. Only need one for each side. But that's not all, cowpokes . . .
CONROY. Whoa. You didn't tell me, uh . . .
MICKEY. Now what is it?
CONROY. Well, this IS the Conroy and Mickey Show, and we DO do it together . . .
MICKEY. We don't spin a record pretty soon there ain't gonna be no *Mickey* and Conroy Show.
CONROY. Now that's the limit — it's my turn!
MICKEY. Yeah, here's a little tune for all you long-distance haulers out there . . . (*Music cuts in. Houselights fade. Lights up on stage and show begins.*) *Insert at end of play, after curtain call: Scrap of a country and western tune segues in and then fades out.*
MICKEY. Mm — yeah, that's a nice one. This is Mickey Miller and . . . (*Waits for Conroy's usual tag but none's forthcoming.*) . . . I said, this is Mickey Miller AND . . . (*Beat.*) Oh fer cryin' out loud! Conroy, you're gonna have to say somethin' sometime. (*Beat.*) Conroy, this is live radio, we're dyin' out here. (*Beat.*) OK, for heaven's sake, OK, OK, you can come down to J.J.'s Feed and Video Rental tonight . . . OK? . . . All right! You can come to the Rustler's Club, too!
CONROY. Throw in the wet T-shirt from the winner?
MICKEY. OK, it's a deal! Now can we do this? This is Mickey Miller . . .
CONROY. AND Conroy Bates . . .
MICKEY. Listen, you all drive real careful out there. (*Cue Music.*)

PROPERTY LIST

Onstage
Beer can
Boulder (large enough to lie on)
Dead lizards
Twigs or tumbleweed, etc.

Offstage
Bags (Shelley)
Orange juice container (Shelley)
Large overstuffed purse or bag (Shelley)
    contains: paperbacks
                  magazines
                  mints
                  can of mace
                  whistle
                  other "useful items for the city dweller"
                  drenched maps
                  tube of heavy sunscreen
                  umbrella
Sun visor (dripping wet with orange juice) (Shelley)
Mirrored sunglasses (Shelley)
People magazine (Shelley)
Towel (Shelley)
Goatskin bag (Ron)

NEW PLAYS

★ **MONTHS ON END by Craig Pospisil.** In comic scenes, one for each month of the year, we follow the intertwined worlds of a circle of friends and family whose lives are poised between happiness and heartbreak. "...a triumph...these twelve vignettes all form crucial pieces in the eternal puzzle known as human relationships, an area in which the playwright displays an assured knowledge that spans deep sorrow to unbounded happiness." –*Ann Arbor News.* "...rings with emotional truth, humor...[an] endearing contemplation on love...entertaining and satisfying." –*Oakland Press.* [5M, 5W] ISBN: 0-8222-1892-5

★ **GOOD THING by Jessica Goldberg.** Brings us into the households of John and Nancy Roy, forty-something high-school guidance counselors whose marriage has been increasingly on the rocks and Dean and Mary, recent graduates struggling to make their way in life. "...a blend of gritty social drama, poetic humor and unsubtle existential contemplation..." –*Variety.* [3M, 3W] ISBN: 0-8222-1869-0

★ **THE DEAD EYE BOY by Angus MacLachlan.** Having fallen in love at their Narcotics Anonymous meeting, Billy and Shirley-Diane are striving to overcome the past together. But their relationship is complicated by the presence of Sorin, Shirley-Diane's fourteen-year-old son, a damaged reminder of her dark past. "...a grim, insightful portrait of an unmoored family..." –*NY Times.* "MacLachlan's play isn't for the squeamish, but then, tragic stories delivered at such an unrelenting fever pitch rarely are." –*Variety.* [1M, 1W, 1 boy] ISBN: 0-8222-1844-5

★ **[SIC] by Melissa James Gibson.** In adjacent apartments three young, ambitious neighbors come together to discuss, flirt, argue, share their dreams and plan their futures with unequal degrees of deep hopefulness and abject despair. "A work...concerned with the sound and power of language..." –*NY Times.* "...a wonderfully original take on urban friendship and the comedy of manners—a *Design for Living* for our times..." –*NY Observer.* [3M, 2W] ISBN: 0-8222-1872-0

★ **LOOKING FOR NORMAL by Jane Anderson.** Roy and Irma's twenty-five-year marriage is thrown into turmoil when Roy confesses that he is actually a woman trapped in a man's body, forcing the couple to wrestle with the meaning of their marriage and the delicate dynamics of family. "Jane Anderson's bittersweet transgender domestic comedy-drama ...is thoughtful and touching and full of wit and wisdom. A real audience pleaser." –*Hollywood Reporter.* [5M, 4W] ISBN: 0-8222-1857-7

★ **ENDPAPERS by Thomas McCormack.** The regal Joshua Maynard, the old and ailing head of a mid-sized, family-owned book-publishing house in New York City, must name a successor. One faction in the house backs a smart, "pragmatic" manager, the other faction a smart, "sensitive" editor and both factions fear what the other's man could do to this house—and to them. "If Kaufman and Hart had undertaken a comedy about the publishing business, they might have written *Endpapers*...a breathlessly fast, funny, and thoughtful comedy ...keeps you amused, guessing, and often surprised...profound in its empathy for the paradoxes of human nature." –*NY Magazine.* [7M, 4W] ISBN: 0-8222-1908-5

★ **THE PAVILION by Craig Wright.** By turns poetic and comic, romantic and philosophical, this play asks old lovers to face the consequences of difficult choices made long ago. "The script's greatest strength lies in the genuineness of its feeling." –*Houston Chronicle.* "Wright's perceptive, gently witty writing makes this familiar situation fresh and thoroughly involving." –*Philadelphia Inquirer.* [2M, 1W (flexible casting)] ISBN: 0-8222-1898-4

DRAMATISTS PLAY SERVICE, INC.
440 Park Avenue South, New York, NY 10016 212-683-8960 Fax 212-213-1539
postmaster@dramatists.com www.dramatists.com

NEW PLAYS

★ **BE AGGRESSIVE by Annie Weisman.** Vista Del Sol is paradise, sandy beaches, avocado-lined streets. But for seventeen-year-old cheerleader Laura, everything changes when her mother is killed in a car crash, and she embarks on a journey to the Spirit Institute of the South where she can learn "cheer" with Bible belt intensity. "...filled with lingual gymnastics...stylized rapid-fire dialogue..." –*Variety*. "...a new, exciting, and unique voice in the American theatre..." –*BackStage West*. [1M, 4W, extras] ISBN: 0-8222-1894-1

★ **FOUR by Christopher Shinn.** Four people struggle desperately to connect in this quiet, sophisticated, moving drama. "...smart, broken-hearted...Mr. Shinn has a precocious and forgiving sense of how power shifts in the game of sexual pursuit...He promises to be a playwright to reckon with..." –*NY Times*. "A voice emerges from an American place. It's got humor, sadness and a fresh and touching rhythm that tell of the loneliness and secrets of life...[a] poetic, haunting play." –*NY Post*. [3M, 1W] ISBN: 0-8222-1850-X

★ **WONDER OF THE WORLD by David Lindsay-Abaire.** A madcap picaresque involving Niagara Falls, a lonely tour-boat captain, a pair of bickering private detectives and a husband's dirty little secret. "Exceedingly whimsical and playfully wicked. Winning and genial. A top-drawer production." –*NY Times*. "Full frontal lunacy is on display. A most assuredly fresh and hilarious tragicomedy of marital discord run amok...absolutely hysterical..." –*Variety*. [3M, 4W (doubling)] ISBN: 0-8222-1863-1

★ **QED by Peter Parnell.** Nobel Prize-winning physicist and all-around genius Richard Feynman holds forth with captivating wit and wisdom in this fascinating biographical play that originally starred Alan Alda. "QED is a seductive mix of science, human affections, moral courage, and comic eccentricity. It reflects on, among other things, death, the absence of God, travel to an unexplored country, the pleasures of drumming, and the need to know and understand." –*NY Magazine*. "Its rhythms correspond to the way that people—even geniuses—approach and avoid highly emotional issues, and it portrays Feynman with affection and awe." –*The New Yorker*. [1M, 1W] ISBN: 0-8222-1924-7

★ **UNWRAP YOUR CANDY by Doug Wright.** Alternately chilling and hilarious, this deliciously macabre collection of four bedtime tales for adults is guaranteed to keep you awake for nights on end. "Engaging and intellectually satisfying...a treat to watch." –*NY Times*. "Fiendishly clever. Mordantly funny and chilling. Doug Wright teases, freezes and zaps us." –*Village Voice*. "Four bite-size plays that bite back." –*Variety*. [flexible casting] ISBN: 0-8222-1871-2

★ **FURTHER THAN THE FURTHEST THING by Zinnie Harris.** On a remote island in the middle of the Atlantic secrets are buried. When the outside world comes calling, the islanders find their world blown apart from the inside as well as beyond. "Harris winningly produces an intimate and poetic, as well as political, family saga." –*Independent (London)*. "Harris' enthralling adventure of a play marks a departure from stale, well-furrowed theatrical terrain." –*Evening Standard (London)*. [3M, 2W] ISBN: 0-8222-1874-7

★ **THE DESIGNATED MOURNER by Wallace Shawn.** The story of three people living in a country where what sort of books people like to read and how they choose to amuse themselves becomes both firmly personal and unexpectedly entangled with questions of survival. "This is a playwright who does not just tell you what it is like to be arrested at night by goons or to fall morally apart and become an aimless yet weirdly contented ghost yourself. He has the originality to make you feel it." –*Times (London)*. "A fascinating play with beautiful passages of writing..." –*Variety*. [2M, 1W] ISBN: 0-8222-1848-8

DRAMATISTS PLAY SERVICE, INC.
440 Park Avenue South, New York, NY 10016 212-683-8960 Fax 212-213-1539
postmaster@dramatists.com www.dramatists.com

NEW PLAYS

★ **SHEL'S SHORTS by Shel Silverstein.** Lauded poet, songwriter and author of children's books, the incomparable Shel Silverstein's short plays are deeply infused with the same wicked sense of humor that made him famous. "...[a] childlike honesty and twisted sense of humor." *–Boston Herald.* "...terse dialogue and an absurdity laced with a tang of dread give [Shel's Shorts] more than a trace of Samuel Beckett's comic existentialism." *–Boston Phoenix.* [flexible casting] ISBN: 0-8222-1897-6

★ **AN ADULT EVENING OF SHEL SILVERSTEIN by Shel Silverstein.** Welcome to the darkly comic world of Shel Silverstein, a world where nothing is as it seems and where the most innocent conversation can turn menacing in an instant. These ten imaginative plays vary widely in content, but the style is unmistakable. "...[An Adult Evening] shows off Silverstein's virtuosic gift for wordplay...[and] sends the audience out...with a clear appreciation of human nature as perverse and laughable." *–NY Times.* [flexible casting] ISBN: 0-8222-1873-9

★ **WHERE'S MY MONEY? by John Patrick Shanley.** A caustic and sardonic vivisection of the institution of marriage, laced with the author's inimitable razor-sharp wit. "...Shanley's gift for acid-laced one-liners and emotionally tumescent exchanges is certainly potent..." *–Variety.* "...lively, smart, occasionally scary and rich in reverse wisdom." *–NY Times.* [3M, 3W] ISBN: 0-8222-1865-8

★ **A FEW STOUT INDIVIDUALS by John Guare.** A wonderfully screwy comedy-drama that figures Ulysses S. Grant in the throes of writing his memoirs, surrounded by a cast of fantastical characters, including the Emperor and Empress of Japan, the opera star Adelina Patti and Mark Twain. "Guare's smarts, passion and creativity skyrocket to awesome heights..." *–Star Ledger.* "...precisely the kind of good new play that you might call an everyday miracle...every minute of it is fresh and newly alive..." *–Village Voice.* [10M, 3W] ISBN: 0-8222-1907-7

★ **BREATH, BOOM by Kia Corthron.** A look at fourteen years in the life of Prix, a Bronx native, from her ruthless girl-gang leadership at sixteen through her coming to maturity at thirty. "...vivid world, believable and eye-opening, a place worthy of a dramatic visit, where no one would want to live but many have to." *–NY Times.* "...rich with humor, terse vernacular strength and gritty detail..." *–Variety.* [1M, 9W] ISBN: 0-8222-1849-6

★ **THE LATE HENRY MOSS by Sam Shepard.** Two antagonistic brothers, Ray and Earl, are brought together after their father, Henry Moss, is found dead in his seedy New Mexico home in this classic Shepard tale. "...His singular gift has been for building mysteries out of the ordinary ingredients of American family life..." *–NY Times.* "...rich moments ...Shepard finds gold." *–LA Times.* [7M, 1W] ISBN: 0-8222-1858-5

★ **THE CARPETBAGGER'S CHILDREN by Horton Foote.** One family's history spanning from the Civil War to WWII is recounted by three sisters in evocative, intertwining monologues. "...bittersweet music—[a] rhapsody of ambivalence...in its modest, garrulous way...theatrically daring." *–The New Yorker.* [3W] ISBN: 0-8222-1843-7

★ **THE NINA VARIATIONS by Steven Dietz.** In this funny, fierce and heartbreaking homage to *The Seagull*, Dietz puts Chekhov's star-crossed lovers in a room and doesn't let them out. "A perfect little jewel of a play..." *–Shepherdstown Chronicle.* "...a delightful revelation of a writer at play; and also an odd, haunting, moving theater piece of lingering beauty." *–Eastside Journal (Seattle).* [1M, 1W (flexible casting)] ISBN: 0-8222-1891-7

DRAMATISTS PLAY SERVICE, INC.
440 Park Avenue South, New York, NY 10016 212-683-8960 Fax 212-213-1539
postmaster@dramatists.com   www.dramatists.com